# The King Who Was Once A Shepherd

**BY MIIKO SHAFFIER**
co-written by Chana Grosser

Illustrated by: Dmitry Gitelman ( diemgi.com )
Layout & Design by: Ken Parker ( visual-variables.com )

Published by:
Shefer Publishing
**www.SheferPublishing.com**

For permissions, comments and ordering information write:
**Miiko@LearnHebrew.tv**

**ISBN 978-1-958999-08-0**

# THE KING
## WHO WAS ONCE A
## SHEPHERD

**an EASY EEVREET STORY**

BY MIIKO SHAFFIER

SHEFER

PUBLISHING

*Based on Samuel 1, Chapter 16, Verses 1-13*
This story can be read like any English story book.
When you get to a Hebrew word, do your best to
sound it out and guess the meaning. You can check the
pronunciation and meaning in the back of the book.

## HAVE FUN!

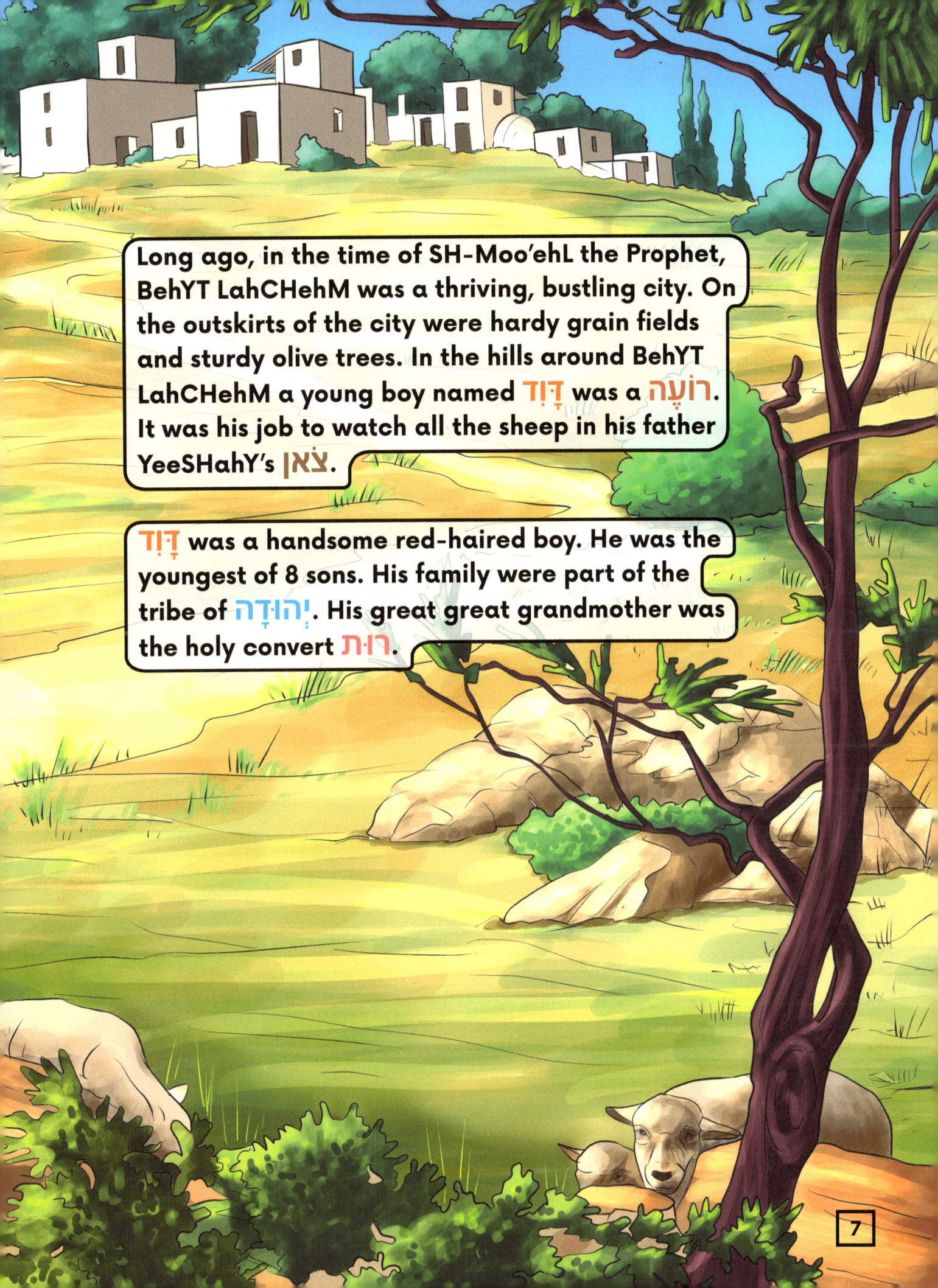

Long ago, in the time of SH-Moo'ehL the Prophet, BehYT LahCHehM was a thriving, bustling city. On the outskirts of the city were hardy grain fields and sturdy olive trees. In the hills around BehYT LahCHehM a young boy named דָּוִד was a רוֹעֶה. It was his job to watch all the sheep in his father YeeSHahY's צֹאן.

דָּוִד was a handsome red-haired boy. He was the youngest of 8 sons. His family were part of the tribe of יְהוּדָה. His great great grandmother was the holy convert רוּת.

While דִוָד was growing and taking care of his father's צֹאן, the king of Israel was King SHah'ooL.

King SHah'ooL had a tremendous responsibility and he didn't always succeed. G-d decided it was time for a new king.

So G-d said to SH-Moo'ehL the Prophet:

"SHah'ooL is no longer fit to be the king of my people. You will go on a special mission to BehYT LahCHehM."

"There," G-d told SH-Moo'ehL, "you will find the next king."

The זִקְנֵי הָעִיר became concerned. What could have happened? What brought SH-Moo'ehL all the way to BehYT LahCHehM?

They rushed out to greet him. "Welcome SH-Moo'ehL! Is everything alright?"

וַיִּקְרָא to YeeSHahY and his sons to join them as well.

As everyone was busy preparing for the festivities SH-Moo'ehL stood ready to anoint the next king of Israel. He looked carefully around and spotted YeeSHahY's son 'ehLeeYahV. 'ehLeeYahV was tall and strong. SH-Moo'ehL thought to himself " 'ehLeeYahV LOOKS like a king!"

But G-d said to SH-Moo'ehL:
"Don't look at 'ehLeeYahV's appearance
or his height. Man sees with his עֵינַיִם.
Only G-d can see deep into a person's
heart and know who he really is."

SH-Moo'ehL looked some more and saw YeeSHahY's second son 'ahVeeYNahDahV. 'ahVeeYNahDahV was handsome and engaging. But G-d told SH-Moo'ehL "He is not the one I בָחַר." Perhaps YeeSHahY's third son SHahMahH was the one?

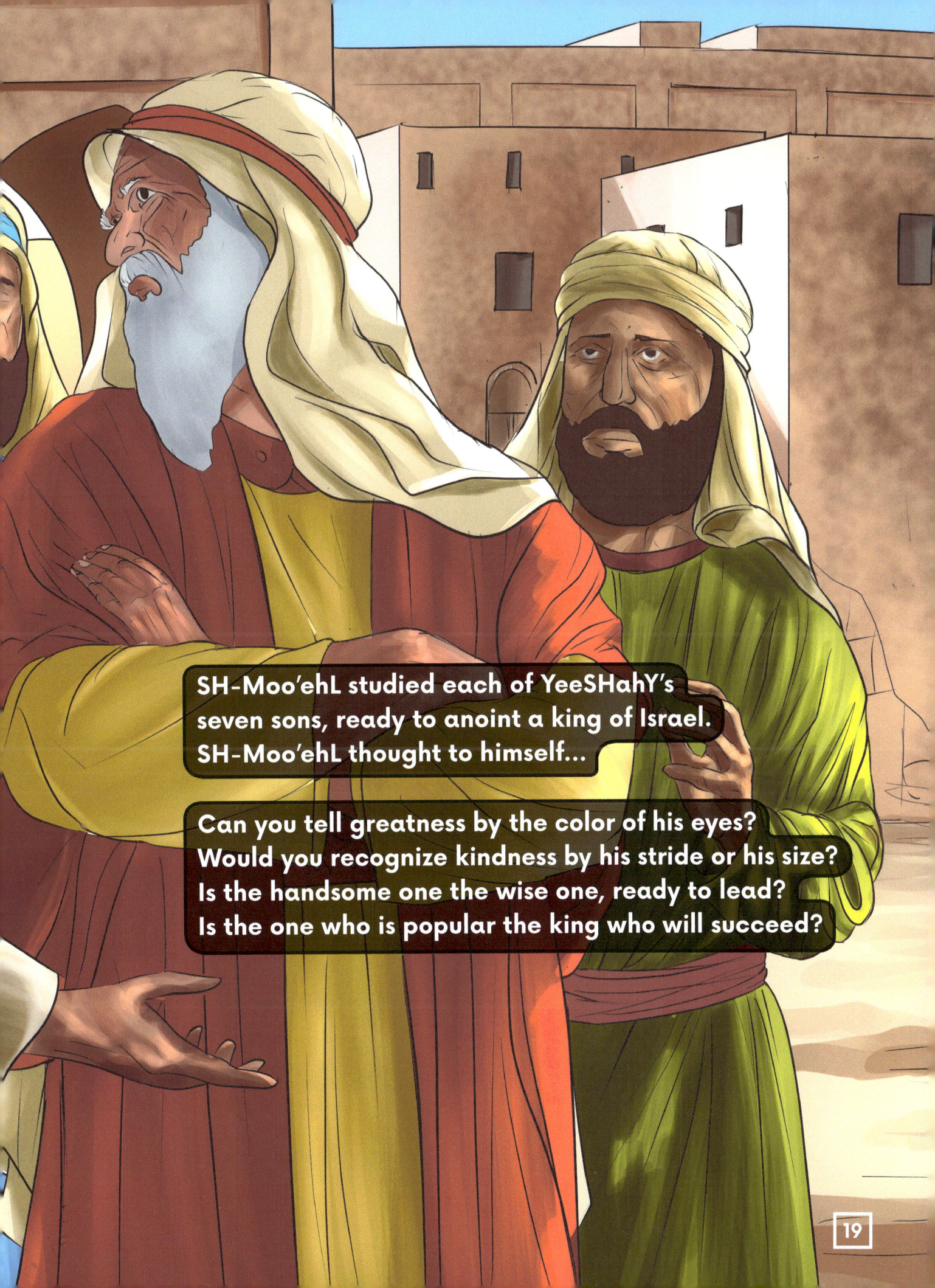

SH-Moo'ehL studied each of YeeSHahY's seven sons, ready to anoint a king of Israel. SH-Moo'ehL thought to himself...

Can you tell greatness by the color of his eyes?
Would you recognize kindness by his stride or his size?
Is the handsome one the wise one, ready to lead?
Is the one who is popular the king who will succeed?

One by one SH-Moo'ehL looked at each of YeeSHahY's wonderful, brave, handsome sons. But none of them was the son G-d בָּחַר.

YeeSHahY answered:

"I have one more son...but he's busy now.
He's the קָטָן, the quiet one anyhow.

You don't need to meet דּוִד.
I can call him...I have no intention to mislead."

"He's lovely! Really he is quite the boy.
He's a רוֹעֶה, a poet, a musician you'd enjoy!

But he can't possibly be the one you are searching
for. Why, he's never even fought in a war."

"Well," said SH-Moo'ehL, "send someone to call him anyway. We won't continue until he comes." YeeSHahY agreed, וַיִּשְׁלַח someone to call דָּוִד, his youngest son.

SH-Moo'ehL was ready! He had a קֶרֶן filled with oil and he poured some of this oil on דָוִד's head. This proclaimed G-d's choice for דָוִד to be king. With דָוִד's family around him, דָוִד was chosen as the next king of Israel.

King דָוִד would bravely lead his people through many מִלְחָמוֹת. He would conquer Y-RooSHahLahYeeM and unite the Tribes of Israel as a nation.

**Here are the Hebrew words from this *Easy Eevreet Story*:**

דָּוִד
DahVeeD - **DAVID**  p. 7,8,22,24,27,28

רוֹעֶה
Roh'ehH - **SHEPHERD**  p. 7,22

צֹאן
TZ'ohN - **FLOCK**  p. 7,8

יְהוּדָה
Y-HooDahH - **JUDAH**  p. 7

רוּת
RooT - **RUTH**  p. 7

זִקְנֵי הָעִיר
ZeeK-NehY Hah'eeYR  p. 12

ZeeK-NehY means **ELDERS** (of) and Hah'eeYR means
**THE CITY**. Together they mean **ELDERS OF THE CITY.**

בָּאתִי
Bah'TeeY - **I CAME**  p. 13

בָּקָר
BahKahR - **CATTLE**  p. 14

| | |
|---|---|
| קוֹרֵא | KohReh' - (HE) CALLS (PRESENT TENSE) |
| קָרָא | KahRah' - (HE) CALLED (PAST TENSE) |
| יִקְרָא | YeeK-Rah' - (HE) WILL CALL (FUTURE TENSE) |

 **וַיִּקְרָא**     VahYeeK-Rah' - **AND (HE) CALLED (PAST TENSE)**   p. 15

Modern Hebrew that's spoken in Israel today is very similar to the Hebrew in the Bible. Of course modern Hebrew has developed new words for new inventions and new ideas. There are also some different grammar rules. Here's an example of a grammar rule you'll find only in biblical Hebrew:

In biblical Hebrew, when you add the prefix **ו** (which means "and") in front of a future tense word like **יִקְרָא** it flips the word from future tense to past tense. It changes the word from "(he) will call" to "and (he) called."

In modern Hebrew the prefix **ו** still means "and" but it doesn't flip a future tense word from future tense to past tense.

 **עֵינַיִם**     'ehYNahYeeM - **EYES**   p. 17

If you want to say only one eye use the word:
**עַיִן** 'ahYeeN **EYE.**

 **בָּחַר**     BahCHahR - **CHOSE**   p. 18,20

Here's another example of how the **I** in front of the word יִשְׁלַח adds the word "and" and also changes the future tense word from future tense to past tense. It changes the word from "(he) will send" to "and (he) sent."

If you want to say one war, use the word:
מִלְחָמָה MeeL-CHahMahH **WAR.**

Awesome reading! Let's take a closer look at one of the Hebrew words we read. Notice how the word can change to mean something a little different.

בָּאתִי     Bah'TeeY - **I CAME**

בָּאתָ     Bah'Tah - **YOU CAME** (one person)

בָּאתֶם     Bah'TehM - **YOU CAME** (more than one person)

בּוֹא     Boh' - **COME** (one person)

בּוֹאוּ     Boh'oo - **COME** (more than one person)

---

You now know some super words. With one of the new words you learned, you can invite someone to join you in a game or just to hang out. Just say בּוֹא! It's a one word invitation and is a favorite among Israelis. If someone needs a little more convincing, the word קוּם is a one word command. It's a serious word so save this one until you really mean it.

# Hi!

My name is **Miiko**. I live in Be'er Sheva, Israel. My husband Aaron and I have nine kids: Menucha, Mendel, Dovi, Yisroel, Freida, Devora, Fitche, Geula, and Azaria.

I teach Hebrew reading with a fun little book called *Learn to Read Hebrew in 6 Weeks!*

My second book *The Hebrew Workbook* teaches readers to write in Hebrew.

*The King Who Was Once a Shepherd* is part of a series of storybooks that teach Hebrew vocabulary to kids.

I'm so pleased to be a part of your Hebrew journey. If you have any questions or want to say hi please send me an email! Miiko@LearnHebrew.tv

# To the Parents

This book is designed to teach Hebrew vocabulary to people who already know how to read the Hebrew alphabet. While reading this Bible story in English you'll come across Hebrew words embedded in the text. Sound out the words and try to guess their meaning from the context. Check the key in the back of the book to see if you were right.

I've chosen to transliterate the names of the biblical characters mentioned in this story so that you'll learn the authentic Hebrew pronunciation of these biblical names.

## Transliteration

*The King Who Was Once a Shepherd* uses the same system of transliteration as my first book *Learn to Read Hebrew in 6 Weeks!*

I came up with a unique transliteration system. It's designed to have the reader pronouncing the Hebrew words accurately without ever having heard a Hebrew speaker pronounce those words.

**Here's a breakdown of the system:**

Each consonant is represented as a capital letter and each vowel by small letters.

The silent letters 'ahLehF (**א**) and 'ahYeeN (**ע**) are represented by an apostrophe (')

The silent vowel 'Sh-Vah' (ְ) is represented as a hyphen (-).

An important exception to make note of:
The CH does not represent the ch sound like in *chair* or *chest*. In fact, Hebrew doesn't have the ch sound like *chair* or *chest* at all.

The CH represents the letters CHehT(**ח**) and CHahF(**כ**) and Final ChahF(**ך**). These letters make a sound not found in the English language. It's a chokey sound that almost sounds like a kitten purring but much harsher. Think about the name of the composer Bach. From what my Spanish speaking students tell me, it's the same sound as the guttural J in Spanish.

Let's look at the first word in the Hebrew Scripture as an example of how my system works:

בְּרֵאשִׁית

I transliterate it:
B-Reh'SHeeYT

Others may transliterate Bereshit or Bresheet but then you wouldn't know if the vowels are long or short.

If you learned to read Hebrew using my other book, you are already well familiar with this system. But in case you learned to read Hebrew elsewhere, here's a key to make sure it's clear.

| א | ב | ב | ג | ד | ה | ו |
|---|---|---|---|---|---|---|
| ' | B | V | G | D | H | V |

| ז | ח | ט | י | כ | כ | ך |
|---|---|---|---|---|---|---|
| Z | CH | T | Y | K | CH | CH |

| ל | מ | מ | נ | ן | ס | ע |
|---|---|---|---|---|---|---|
| L | M | M | N | N | S | ' |

| ר | ק | צ | ץ | פ | פ | ף |
|---|---|---|---|---|---|---|
| R | K | TZ | TZ | F | F | P |

| ש | ת | ת |
|---|---|---|
| SH | T | T |

| דַ | וֹ | וֹ | וּ | וֶ | וָ |
|---|---|---|---|---|---|
| - | ee | oh | oo | eh | ah |

# LEARN TO READ AND WRITE **HEBREW** WITH MY FUN AND EASY SYSTEM!

## #1 BESTSELLERS
IN HEBREW LANGUAGE INSTRUCTION

- FUN MEMORY TRICKS
- 12 SIMPLE LESSONS
- PACED TO FINISH IN 6 WEEKS
- LEARN TO READ THE HEBREW BIBLE
- GREAT FOR ADULTS OR CHILDREN ALIKE
- CHARMING ILLUSTRATIONS TO MAKE LEARNING HEBREW A PLEASURE

**MORE DETAILS AT LEARNHEBREW.TV**

AVAILABLE AT AMAZON

www.ingramcontent.com/pod-product-compliance
Lightning Source LLC
Chambersburg PA
CBHW041436120626
46547CB00002B/244